S0-ECZ-975

God
Wash
the
World
and
Start
Again

God
Wash
the
World
and
Start
Again

by Lorenz Graham · Pictures by Clare Romano Ross

Thomas Y. Crowell Company, New York

By the Author

Every Man Heart Lay Down

God Wash the World and Start Again

A Road down in the Sea

These little poems . . . are told here in the words and
thought patterns of a modern African boy who does not . . .
use the conventional words and phrases which by long
usage often obscure the meaning of these tales in the
minds of Europeans and Americans.
This is the stuff of which literature is made . . . .
—W. E. B. Du Bois

From the Foreword of *How God Fix Jonah*, the original
collection of stories from the Bible retold by Lorenz
Graham, in which GOD WASH THE WORLD AND START AGAIN first appeared.

Introduction

The familiar Bible stories of kings and slaves, of strength and weakness, of love and hate were brought to Africa by missionaries. As they were retold by Africans, they took on the imagery of the people. Shepherd David with his harp of many strings, strong man Samson who was weak for woman palaver, and baby Jesus born in the place where cattle sleep are now part of the folklore of the country. To the African storyteller the Bible tale becomes a poem, or rather a spoken song. His words are simple and rhythmic. The song is sung, and it is sweet.

It was in Liberia that I first heard many of these tales, recounted in the idiom of Africans newly come to English speech. They can be heard in many other parts of the continent as well—in the west and even in the east, wherever the English settlers spread their language.

Words of Spanish and Portuguese still remain on the African coast. *Palaver* now means something more than *palabra*, or "word." It can mean business or discussion or trouble. When "war palaver catch the country," people must fight, and some must die; and "woman palaver" often lands a man in jail. *Pican*, for baby or son or child, comes from *pequeño* ("small") and *niño* ("child"). The two words flowed together in English speech to become first *picaninny* and then *pican*.

Read again an old story. Behold a new vision with sharper images. Sway with the rhythm of the storyteller. Feel the beat of the drums:

Long time past
Before you papa live
Before him papa live
Before him pa's papa live——

Long time past
Before them big tree live
Before them big tree's papa live——
That time God live.

You talking bout the time!
You think you see some rain!
You vex to see the water falling so
On the house!

God make the time for Him Own Self.
He make the rain
He make the dry and wet.
He make the sunny day
And dark of night for rest.
This time He make it good for we
And rainy day can come and go
And all be dry again
And people live.

But was a time
When all the world be young,
And so-so long time past,
That God let all the rain fall down
And cover up the land
And every house and tree
And every hill and mountain.
The rain done fall that time for true.

First time God make the world
And all the mens
And all the thing that move about.
First time Him heart lay down
But bye-m-bye He look and see
The people no be fit to hear Him Word
And things what walk be bad too much
And God want try again.

God see mens what grow like trees
And elephants like mountains walk about
And leopards big like elephant

And monkey mens what eat the people
And snakes what carry fire in their mouth
To cook the mens they eat.

And God no like to see
the world be so.

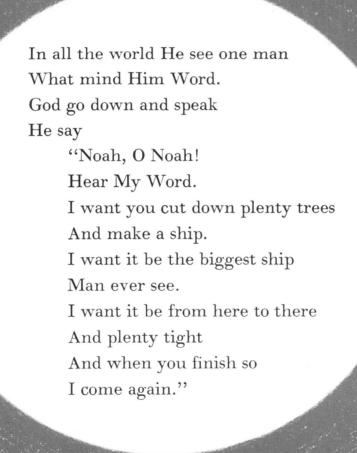

In all the world He see one man
What mind Him Word.
God go down and speak
He say
    "Noah, O Noah!
    Hear My Word.
    I want you cut down plenty trees
    And make a ship.
    I want it be the biggest ship
    Man ever see.
    I want it be from here to there
    And plenty tight
    And when you finish so
    I come again."

Now Noah call him people,
All him sons and all the mens they got.
They set to cut down trees
And lay to build a ship
And people come and laugh.
They say
　　　"How now?
　　　This old man Noah build him ship
　　　Far from the sea.
　　　How now?
　　　Who going carry ship to water for him
　　　When he finish?
　　　He be fool!"

The people come and laugh
But Noah and him people build
And make it tight with pitch.
God come walk about inside the ship
And Noah hear God's Word and mind.
God say like this
      "Noah, O Noah,
      You make it here rooms
      And here you make a cargo space
      Just so."
Nother time God say
      "Noah, O Noah,
      That side you got bad board,
      Make it your son take that one out."

And how God say, that way Old Noah do.
One day the ship be finish
All the people come to see.
The ship be big past anything before
And no water there.

God walk about with Noah on the ship.
He say
"Noah, O Noah,
You hear My Word
You make My heart lay down.

Now see what you must do.
Go take up in all the land
The things what walk

The things what crawl
The things what fly
Go catch them two by two."

So Noah call him people,
And him sons and all the mens they got,
They set to bring the living things
That walk and crawl and fly
They bring the man and woman kind
They bring them two by two.
They bring in corn and rice for chop.
They bring in elephant
They bring in cow and horse
And fowl and snake and goat
And dog and leopard,
Deer and monkey
And everything that move in bush
And in the air
They bring.
And God look on and call for something else
And something else they bring.
And God look on and know
The thing be good.

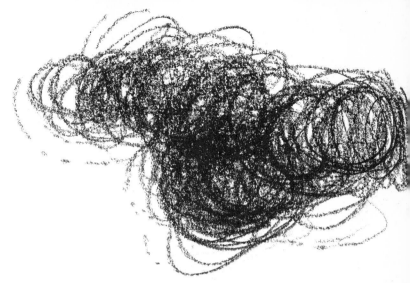

He say
  "Noah, O Noah,
  You done mind me good!
  Now go aboard and take you people,
  Seal the door and seal the hatch
  And wait!"

That time God open up the sky

And let the water fall

And all the world see water.

It no fall in rain that time

It pour down till all the world be full.

And rivers run in every road

And every field be like a lake

And every lake be like a sea

And all the low land fill.

And hills stand up like islands

And then the islands self done cover

And only mountains stand.

And soon the mountains cover up

And all the land and all the sea be all the same.

Where be the people what done laugh?
Where be the giants what walk like trees?
Where be the leopards big like elephants?
And all the elephants standing up like mountains?
Where they be?

God look down on all the water
And then He hold the rain.
God look down and all he find
Be Noah's one ship on the sea.
In that one ship live everything that live
Above the water.

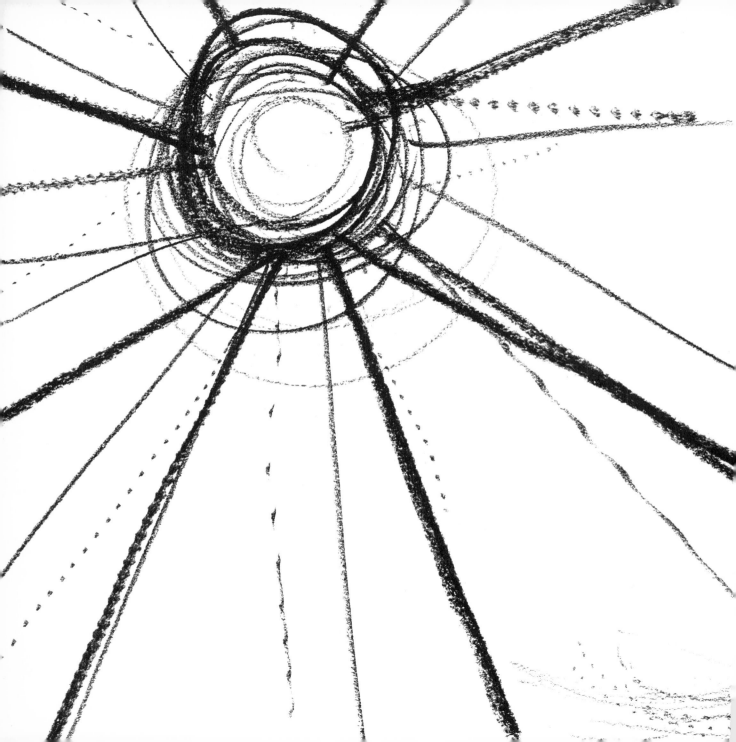

God say
  "Now!
  My old world done finish.
  I make new start
  And everything I do
  I look him good."

God open new holes down in the sea
To drain the land.
He make the sun shine bright
And send dry winds
To sweep the world.

He put the ship down softly
And see Noah with His people
And all the things that walk
And things what crawl
And things what fly
Go out again.

He smile
And in the sky He set Him bow
And turn to make a better world.

About the Author

Lorenz Graham was born in New Orleans, Louisiana, the son of a
Methodist minister. He attended the University of California at Los
Angeles for three years, then went to Africa to teach in a Liberian
mission school.

Mr. Graham became interested in the tribal culture of his students
and wanted to write about the African people. He returned to the
United States and was graduated from Virginia Union University.
Later he did postgraduate work at the New York School for Social
Work and at New York University. He has worked with young people
as a teacher and a social worker.

The author met his wife in Liberia, where she also was a teacher.
They make their home in southern California and have traveled
extensively in Africa and the Far East. Most of Mr. Graham's time
is now given to writing.

About the Artist

Clare Romano Ross is a graduate of the Cooper Union School of Art
and studied at the Ecole des Beaux Arts at Fontainebleau, France, and
the Instituto Statale in Florence, Italy. She lived in Italy for a
year on a Fulbright grant and was also a recipient of a Tiffany
fellowship for printmaking. Clare Romano Ross and her artist husband,
John Ross, were artists in residence with the USIA exhibition "Graphic
Arts, U.S.A." in Yugoslavia.

Mrs. Ross is represented in museums throughout the United
States, and her work is in the permanent collection of the Metropolitan
Museum of Art and the Library of Congress. She is also on the faculty of
Pratt Institute and the New School for Social Research.